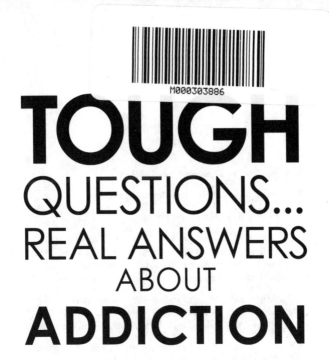

TOUGH
QUESTIONS...
REAL ANSWERS
ABOUT
ADDICTION

SMITH
FREEMAN
Publishing

Tough Questions...Real Answers About Addiction

Bible verses were taken from the following translations:

ISBN: 978-0-9986529-2-4

Contents

A Message to Readers

In the twentieth chapter of Exodus, God warns, "You shall have no other gods before Me" (v. 3 NKJV). Yet people who suffer from the ravages of addiction are constantly forced to choose between putting God first or succumbing to the urges that enslave them. More often than not, the urges win, with devastating consequences.

Perhaps you're considering treatment for yourself. Or perhaps you believe a family member or friend needs help. In either case, this book was written for you, a Christian who's looking for real answers to some very tough questions.

This text does not attempt to answer every specific question concerning every type of addiction or every specific treatment methodology. Instead, it gives time-tested, Biblically based strategies to help addicts heal their hearts by healing their addictions.

Addiction is not a sign of weakness or an indication of God's displeasure. It is an illness, a readably treatable condition that should never be ignored. If this book assists you, even in a small way, as you or your loved one seeks treatment, it will have served its purpose. May God bless you and keep you, and may He place His healing hand upon you and your loved ones, now and forever.

Christ is victorious over addiction.

GERALD MAY, MD

Five Things to Remember about Addiction

It's not just drugs and alcohol. Certain behaviors can be addictive too.

It's a physical disease. As the addiction progresses, brain chemistry changes and the brain itself changes, thus making it increasingly difficult for the addict to abstain from the drug or addictive behavior.

Treatment is available. If you want it, you can find it. And many options, such as twelve-step programs, are free.

It's possible to recover. Millions have done it; so can you. With God, all things are possible.

God's grace is bigger than your addiction. The Lord can heal your pain, and He can heal your addiction if you admit your helplessness, turn everything over to Him, and utilize the treatment opportunities He places along your path.

1

The Question

It seems like addictive substances are everywhere. How common is addiction?

The Answer

Modern society is permeated with addictive substances, some of which are legal and many of which are not. Your job is to avoid the world's temptations and obey your Father in heaven.

For the power of addiction to be overcome, human will must act in concert with divine will.

GERALD MAY, MD

The Addictive Society

Let us walk with decency, as in the daylight:
not in carousing and drunkenness.
ROMANS 13:13 HCSB

Whether you realize it or not, you live in an addictive society. You inhabit a world in which addictions are thoroughly woven into the fabric of everyday life, a society where alcohol is ubiquitous and drugs (prescription or otherwise) are readily available. In your world, behavioral addictions have more outlets than ever before: Gambling is sanctioned—and often marketed—by state governments; Internet-fed addictions are only a few clicks away; and food addictions have reached epidemic proportions. And despite the "war on drugs," drug addiction and alcoholism continue to plague our nation and the world.

Because you're surrounded by addictive behaviors, you may be tempted to take them for granted, convincing yourself that "everybody does it" or that "it's not really a problem." Such thinking is not only wrong; it's also in direct conflict with the basic tenets of the Christian faith. Addictions destroy lives, families, and careers. Addictions cause smart people to do foolish things, healthy people to forfeit their health, and sane people to lose their sanity. And of course addictive behaviors often lead to criminality, eventually costing many addicts their freedom.

Ours is a society that often glamorizes the use of drugs, alcohol, cigarettes, and other addictive substances. Why? The answer can be summed up in one word: money. Simply put, addictive substances are incredibly profitable, so suppliers (of both legal and illegal substances) work overtime to make certain that potential customers sample their products. The suppliers continue to market their products, at least in part, because they need a steady stream of new addicts because the old ones continue to perish prematurely.

God's values and the world's values are seldom the same. Although we live in the world, we must not worship it. Although we live in an addictive society, we must avoid the substances and behaviors that threaten to enslave us. And when we find ourselves trapped in the web of addiction, we must take all necessary steps to escape.

More Thoughts about Addiction

Some of the most heart-breaking letters I receive are from people who tell how alcohol or drugs have ravaged their lives and destroyed their families.

BILLY GRAHAM

The Bible condemns any substance which alters or distorts our thinking, including alcohol, which was the most common drug of ancient times.

BILLY GRAHAM

Wine hath drowned more men than the sea.

THOMAS FULLER

No matter how many pleasures Satan offers you,
his ultimate intention is to ruin you.
Your destruction is his highest priority.

ERWIN LUTZER

We first make our habits, then our habits make us.

JOHN DRYDEN

Some Facts about
Addiction to Alcohol

Alcohol is the most commonly used addictive substance in the United States: 17.6 million people, or one in every twelve adults, suffer from alcohol abuse or dependence, along with several million more who engage in risky binge drinking patterns that could lead to alcohol problems.

In the United States, approximately 88,000 deaths annually are attributed to excessive alcohol use.

Up to 40 percent of all hospital beds in the United States (except for those being used by maternity and intensive care patients) are being used to treat health conditions that are directly or indirectly related to alcohol consumption.

NATIONAL COUNCIL ON ALCOHOL AND DRUG DEPENDENCE

2

The Question

What, exactly, is addiction?

The Answer

Addiction is a complex condition, a brain disease that is characterized by compulsive substance use despite harmful consequences. People with addiction have an intense focus on using a certain substance, such as alcohol or drugs, to the point that it takes over their lives. Addicts continue using alcohol or drugs even when they know it will causes problems.

AMERICAN PSYCHOLOGICAL ASSOCIATION

Is your relationship with alcohol or drugs affecting any area of your life in a significantly negative way? Have you tried, but failed, to abstain? If so, your behavior can be described as addictive.

DOUGLAS COOK, MD

Addiction Is Slavery

Worship the Lord your God, and serve only Him.
MATTHEW 4:10 HCSB

The dictionary defines addiction as "the compulsive need for a habit-forming substance; the condition of being habitually and compulsively occupied with something." That definition is accurate but incomplete. For Christians, addiction has an additional meaning: It means compulsively worshipping something other than God.

The word "addiction" is derived from the Latin word *addicere*, which means to give over or surrender one's rights to someone else. Addiction occurs when someone becomes enslaved to alcohol, to drugs, or to an addictive behavior.

Addiction is a cruel taskmaster. It seizes lives and sows destruction. When it does, well-intentioned men and women live in denial for years while their addictive behaviors disrupt families and destroy lives. The addiction becomes the master; the addict becomes the slave. As the addiction assumes more and more control over the addict's thoughts and actions, self-control progressively deteriorates as the addiction seizes control of chemical functions in the brain. Normal mechanisms of learning and memory are hijacked. It is not until a person experiments with an addictive substance or behavior that he can know how he will respond. It's an insidious cruelty of addiction that the addict doesn't know he's been trapped until he's already enslaved.

If you or someone you love is suffering from the blight of addiction, remember this: Help is available. Many people have experienced addiction and lived to tell about it, so never abandon hope. With God, all things are possible. And if you're one of those fortunate people who hasn't started experimenting with addictive substances, congratulations. You have just have spared yourself a lifetime of headaches and heartaches.

More from God's Word

I have told you these things so that in Me you may have peace. You will have suffering in this world. Be courageous! I have conquered the world.
JOHN 16:33 HCSB

*I have heard your prayer;
I have seen your tears. Look, I will heal you.*
2 KINGS 20:5 HCSB

We are hard-pressed on every side, yet not crushed; we are perplexed, but not in despair.
2 CORINTHIANS 4:8 NKJV

I called to the LORD in my distress; I called to my God. From His temple He heard my voice.
2 SAMUEL 22:7 HCSB

God blesses those who patiently endure testing and temptation. Afterward they will receive the crown of life that God has promised to those who love him.

JAMES 1:12 NLT

About Drug Addiction

Drug addiction, also called substance use disorder, is a dependence on a legal or illegal drug or medication. Keep in mind that alcohol and nicotine are legal substances but are also considered drugs.

MAYO CLINIC

People with a substance use disorder have distorted thinking, behavior, and body functions. Changes in the brain's wiring are what cause people to have intense cravings for the drug and make it hard to stop using the drug. Brain imaging studies show changes in the areas of the brain that relate to judgment, decision making, learning, memory, and behavior control.

AMERICAN PSYCHOLOGICAL ASSOCIATION

Addiction is a chronic, often relapsing brain disease that causes compulsive drug seeking and use, despite harmful consequences to the addicted individual and to those around him or her. Although the initial decision to take drugs is voluntary for most people, the brain changes that occur over time challenge an addicted person's self-control and hamper his or her ability to resist intense impulses to take drugs.

NATIONAL COUNCIL ON ALCOHOL AND DRUG DEPENDENCE

3

The Question

What about other addictions, like gambling?

The Answer

Addictions come in two general types:
chemical addictions and "process" addictions.
The chemical addictions include alcohol,
cigarettes, and drugs. Process addictions
include such behaviors as compulsive gambling,
sexual addiction, eating disorders,
and compulsive spending.

*A Christian is held captive by anything
that hinders the abundant and effective
Spirit-filled life God planned for him or her.*

BETH MOORE

So Many Types of Addiction

Be strong and courageous, and do the work.
Don't be afraid or discouraged,
for the LORD God, my God, is with you.
He won't leave you or forsake you.
1 CHRONICLES 28:20 HCSB

Drugs. Alcohol. Gambling. Sexual addiction. Internet addiction. Compulsive spending. And the list goes on. In modern society, addictive substances and behaviors are woven into the fabric of cultural life. Try as we might, we simply cannot escape them. So unless you're living on a deserted island, you know people who are full-blown addicts—probably lots of people. If you, or someone you love, is suffering from the blight of addiction, the following ideas are worth remembering:

1. For the addict, addiction comes first. In the life of an addict, addiction rules. God, of course, commands otherwise (Exodus 20:3). Our task, as believers, is to put God in His proper place: first place.

2. You cannot cure another person's addiction, but you can encourage that person to seek help. Addicts are cured when they decide, not when you decide. What you can do is this: You can be supportive, and you can encourage the addict to find the help that he or she needs (Luke 10:25–37).

3. If you are living with an addicted person, think about safety: yours and your family's. Addiction is life-threatening and life-shortening. Don't let someone else's addiction threaten your safety or the safety of your loved ones (Proverbs 22:3).

4. Don't assist in prolonging the addiction. When you interfere with the negative consequences that might otherwise

accompany an addict's negative behaviors, you are inadvertently "enabling" the addict to continue the destructive cycle of addiction. So don't be an enabler (Proverbs 15:31).

5. Help is available. Many people have experienced addiction and survived. They want to help. Let them (Proverbs 27:17).

6. Cure is possible. With God's help, no addiction is incurable. And with God, no situation is hopeless (Matthew 19:26).

More from God's Word

He heals the brokenhearted
and binds up their wounds.
PSALM 147:3 HCSB

Weeping may endure for a night,
but joy cometh in the morning.
PSALM 30:5 KJV

The LORD shall give thee rest from thy sorrow,
and from thy fear.
ISAIAH 14:3 KJV

The LORD is near to those who have a broken heart.
PSALM 34:18 NKJV

Ye shall be sorrowful, but your sorrow
shall be turned into joy.
JOHN 16:20 KJV

About Addiction

Over 50,000 Americans die each year from overdoses of prescription and illegal drugs. Prescription drugs account for over half of these deaths.

NATIONAL CENTER ON HEALTH STATISTICS, VDV

Abusing drugs or alcohol before the brain is fully developed, anytime before a person's mid-twenties, may increase the risk for addiction later in life due to the changes these substances make to growing brains.

THE JOURNAL OF CLINICAL EEG AND NEUROSCIENCE

Approximately one out of every twelve American teenagers suffers from a substance abuse disorder.

NATIONAL SURVEY ON DRUG USE AND HEALTH

Approximately one out of every six American young adults (between the ages of eighteen and twenty-five) has a substance-use disorder. This represents the highest percentage of any age group (approximately 16 percent).

NATIONAL SURVEY ON DRUG USE AND HEALTH

The same kind of kind of brain functions that apply to substance abuse also apply to non-substance addictions. Whether it's addiction to money, power, or some particular behavior, the patterns of feedback and conditioning are similar. The exact systems of nerve cells may be different, but the patterns are the same.

GERALD MAY, MD

4

The Question

Is addiction merely a personal weakness,
or is it a physical illness?

The Answer

Addiction is a physical disease. As the addiction
progresses, the brain physically changes, thus
making it increasingly difficult for the addict to
abstain from the drug or the addictive behavior.

*Complete abstinence is easier
than perfect moderation.*

St. Augustine

Addiction Is a Physical Disease

The disease of addiction, like other diseases, is chronic and organic. It cites the brain as its target organ. It relapses. It remits. It is cunning, baffling, and powerful, but treated one day at a time, lasting recovery is the promise for each and every alcoholic or addict afflicted. All that is required is that they have the willingness to take the first steps.

HAZELDEN BETTY FORD FOUNDATION

For millennia, addiction was viewed as a sign of weakness, or self-indulgence, or a lack of moral fiber. No more. Today, thanks to cutting-edge research, we know that the process of addiction causes physical changes in the brain that have a profound impact on thought and behavior:

Addiction is a disease that targets the organ known as the mid-brain. The cause is regulatory dysfunction of a neurotransmitter called dopamine. The effect is a common group of symptoms seen in each and every alcoholic and addict known to have the disease of dependence: a loss of control, craving, and persistent use despite adverse consequences. Many alcoholics and addicts have been accused of selfishness, of choosing their behaviors for a reward or pleasure. This impression—of hedonistic behavior on the part of the addict—causes inappropriate judgment, bringing unwarranted shame to the one who suffers with this disease.

HAZELDEN BETTY FORD FOUNDATION

So whether you're helping a loved one seek treatment or considering treatment for yourself, it's important to realize that addiction is an illness, not a weakness—and it should be treated accordingly.

Groundbreaking discoveries about the brain have revolutionized our understanding of addiction, enabling us to respond effectively to the problem. We now know that addiction is a disease that affects both brain and behavior. We have identified many of the biological and environmental factors and are beginning to search for the genetic variations that contribute to the development and progression of the disease.

Nora Volkow, MD, Director, National Institute of Drug Abuse

More from God's Word

And so, dear brothers and sisters, I plead with you to give your bodies to God because of all he has done for you. Let them be a living and holy sacrifice—the kind he will find acceptable. This is truly the way to worship him.

Romans 12:1 NLT

Do not let sin reign in your mortal body, so that you obey its desires.

Romans 6:12 HCSB

You made them only a little lower than God and crowned them with glory and honor.

Psalm 8:5 NLT

How Drugs Work

Drugs are chemicals that tap into the brain's communication system and disrupt the way nerve cells normally send, receive, and process information. Drugs cause this disruption: by imitating the brain's natural chemical messengers or by overstimulating the "reward circuitry" of the brain.

Nearly all drugs, directly or indirectly, target the brain's reward system by flooding the circuit with dopamine. Dopamine is a neurotransmitter—a chemical messenger—present in regions of the brain that control movement, emotion, motivation, and feelings of pleasure. The overstimulation of this system produces euphoric effects in response to the drugs. This reaction sets in motion a pattern that "teaches" people to repeat the behavior of abusing drugs.

As a person continues to abuse drugs, the brain adapts to the dopamine surges by producing less dopamine or reducing the number of dopamine receptors. The user must therefore keep abusing drugs to bring his or her dopamine function back to "normal" or use more drugs to achieve a dopamine high.

Long-term drug abuse causes changes in other brain chemical systems and circuits. Brain imaging studies of drug-addicted individuals show changes in areas of the brain that are critical to judgment, decision making, learning and memory, and behavior control. Together, these changes can drive an abuser to seek out and take drugs compulsively—in other words, to become addicted to drugs.

NATIONAL COUNCIL ON ALCOHOL AND DRUG DEPENDENCE

5

The Question

Are drugs and alcohol really dangerous,
or is it an exaggeration?

The Answer

The use of drugs and alcohol often leads to
addiction, which is a serious chronic illness. People
who experiment with addictive substances are
inevitably taking the risk that they, too, may
become addicted. So there can be no debate:
Drugs and alcohol are dangerous substances that
often lead to ill health or even death.

—⁂—

*The alcoholic commits suicide
on the installment plan.*

VANCE HAVNER

Principles of
Effective Treatment

*Each generation becomes more addicted
to the sedatives of life, to dull the pain of living.*
BILLY GRAHAM

Based on scientific research conducted since the mid-1970s, the following key principles should form the basis of any effective treatment program:

- Addiction is a complex but treatable disease that affects brain function and behavior.
- Medically assisted detoxification is only the first stage of treatment.
- No single treatment is right for everyone.
- Effective treatment addresses all of the patient's needs, not just his or her drug use.
- Staying in treatment long enough is critical.
- Counseling and other behavioral therapies are the most commonly used forms of treatment.
- Medications are often an important part of treatment, especially when combined with behavioral therapies.
- Treatment plans must be reviewed often and modified to fit the patient's changing needs.
- Treatment should address other possible mental disorders.
- Treatment doesn't need to be voluntary to be effective.
- Drug use during treatment must be monitored continuously.

NATIONAL INSTITUTE OF DRUG ABUSE

More from God's Word

Let us lay aside every weight and the sin that so easily ensnares us. Let us run with endurance the race that lies before us, keeping our eyes on Jesus, the source and perfecter of our faith.

HEBREWS 12:1–2 HCSB

Take heed, brethren, lest there be in any of you an evil heart of unbelief, in departing from the living God. But exhort one another daily, while it is called To day; lest any of you be hardened through the deceitfulness of sin.

HEBREWS 3:12–13 KJV

Don't be deceived: God is not mocked. For whatever a man sows he will also reap, because the one who sows to his flesh will reap corruption from the flesh, but the one who sows to the Spirit will reap eternal life from the Spirit.

GALATIANS 6:7–8 HCSB

Therefore submit to God. Resist the devil and he will flee from you. Draw near to God and He will draw near to you. Cleanse your hands, you sinners; and purify your hearts, you double-minded.

JAMES 4:7–8 NKJV

Little children, let no one deceive you! The one who does what is right is righteous, just as He is righteous.

1 JOHN 3:7 HCSB

Facts about Addiction

Beyond the negative consequences for the individual, drug abuse and addiction have a significant impact on society at large. Estimates of the total overall costs of substance abuse in the United States, including productivity and health- and crime-related costs, exceed $600 billion annually. This includes approximately $193 billion for illicit drugs, $193 billion for tobacco, and $235 billion for alcohol. As staggering as these numbers are, they do not fully describe the breadth of destructive public health and safety implications of drug abuse and addiction, such as family disintegration, loss of employment, failure in school, domestic violence, and child abuse.

NATIONAL COUNCIL ON ALCOHOL AND DRUG DEPENDENCE

About half of the population of American prisons and jails suffer from addiction.

NATIONAL SURVEY ON DRUG USE AND HEALTH

In the United States, more than half of all adults have a family history of alcoholism or problem drinking, and more than 7 million children live in a household where at least one parent is dependent on or has abused alcohol.

NATIONAL COUNCIL ON ALCOHOL AND DRUG DEPENDENCE

6

The Question

It seems like my world is filled with distractions
and temptations. What should I do?

The Answer

You live in a society that's brimming with
distractions and temptations. Everywhere you turn,
you're confronted with them. Your job is to steer
clear of worldly distractions and focus, instead,
on God and His plan for your life.

Temptation is the starting point of addiction.

GERALD MAY, MD

Beware the Enemy

*Your adversary, the devil, prowls around like
a roaring lion, seeking someone to devour.*

1 Peter 5:8 NASB

This world can be a dangerous place, especially if you're suffering from an addiction. Enticements are everywhere. Even if you think you're in a very safe place today, be careful. Whether you realize it or not, your adversary—the addiction—is always nearby, waiting for an opening, ready to strike you down if you drop your guard. The enemy has no pity, no compassion, and no remorse. And because he's far stronger than you, he'll eventually destroy you if you try to fight him singlehandedly.

Never before in the entire history of humankind have adults and children alike been offered access to so many spiritual snares. Never before has the devil had so many tools. So beware. Take a stand against your enemy. And ask for God's protection. Because your adversary never takes a day off...and neither should you.

More from God's Word

Do not be misled: "Bad company
corrupts good character."
1 CORINTHIANS 15:33 NIV

Let us lay aside every weight, and the sin which
so easily ensnares us, and let us run with endurance
the race that is set before us.
HEBREWS 12:1 NKJV

Encourage each other daily, while it is still called
today, so that none of you is hardened by sin's
deception.
HEBREWS 3:13 HCSB

No temptation has overtaken you but such
as is common to man; and God is faithful,
who will not allow you to be tempted beyond
what you are able, but with the temptation
will provide the way of escape.
1 CORINTHIANS 10:13 NASB

Put on the whole armor of God, that you may
be able to stand against the wiles of the devil.
EPHESIANS 6:11 NKJV

More Thoughts about Temptation

*It is easier to stay out of temptation
than to get out of it.*

RICK WARREN

*Temptations that have been anticipated,
guarded against, and prayed about have
little power to harm us. Jesus tells us to
"keep watching and praying,
that you may not come into temptation."*

JOHN MACARTHUR

*It is not the temptations you have, but the decision
you make about them, that counts.*

BILLY GRAHAM

*The first step on the way to victory
is to recognize the enemy.*

CORRIE TEN BOOM

*Every temptation, directly or indirectly,
is the temptation to doubt and distrust God.*

JOHN MACARTHUR

7

The Question

Peer pressure is everywhere, and some people
are constantly encouraging me to do things
I don't believe in. What should I do?

The Answer

The world is full of temptations and some people
will encourage you to give in. Since you can't
please everybody, you're better off trying
to please God.

*Remember that your character
is the sum total of your habits.*

RICK WARREN

Addiction Tears
Down Character

The integrity of the upright guides them,
but the perversity of the treacherous destroys them.
PROVERBS 11:3 HCSB

Addiction inevitably destroys character. And that's a problem. God's Word makes it clear that integrity matters to Him, so it must matter to us as well. If we wish to walk in the light of God's truth, we must be truthful. Honesty enriches life; deception and addiction destroy it.

It has been said on many occasions and in many ways that honesty is the best policy. But it's far more important to note that honesty is God's policy. And it's also worth noting that you'll respect yourself more when you make a rock-solid commitment to be a person of integrity.

Sometime soon, perhaps even today, you will be tempted to bend the truth or perhaps even to break it. And if you're an addict, you'll probably have the opportunity to twist the truth as it relates to your addiction. Resist that temptation. Truth is God's way, and it must be your way, too. Living a life of integrity isn't the easiest way, but it's always the best way. And it's also the best way to get sober and stay sober.

More from God's Word

The godly are directed by honesty.
PROVERBS 11:5 NLT

*Let integrity and uprightness preserve me,
for I wait for You.*
PSALM 25:21 NKJV

*The godly walk with integrity;
blessed are their children who follow them.*
PROVERBS 20:7 NLT

*Whoever walks in integrity walks securely,
but whoever takes crooked paths will be found out.*
PROVERBS 10:9 NIV

*He stores up success for the upright;
He is a shield for those who live with integrity.*
PROVERBS 2:7 HCSB

More Thoughts about Character

*Maintaining your integrity in a world of sham
is no small accomplishment.*

WAYNE OATES

*True greatness is not measured by the headlines
or wealth. The inner character of a person
is the true measure of lasting greatness.*

BILLY GRAHAM

Character is built over a lifetime.

ELIZABETH GEORGE

Character is what you are in the dark.

D. L. MOODY

*Let your words be the genuine picture
of your heart.*

JOHN WESLEY

8

The Question

I've behaved badly at times, and I'm ashamed of the things I've done. What should I do?

The Answer

First, be certain that you're no longer doing the thing that caused your guilt in the first place. Then, ask for forgiveness (from God and from anybody you've hurt). Next, make sure you forgive yourself. And finally, if you still have residual feelings of bitterness or regret, keep asking God to heal your heart. When you ask, He will answer in His own time and in His own way.

The purpose of guilt is to bring us to Jesus. Once we are there, then its purpose is finished. If we continue to make ourselves guilty— to blame ourselves—then that is a sin in itself.

CORRIE TEN BOOM

Beyond Guilt and Shame

Blessed is the one who does not condemn himself.
ROMANS 14:22 NIV

Addiction and shame are traveling companions. In the course of the disease, the addict inevitably does things that cause feelings of inadequacy and regret. But God has an answer for the shame and the guilt. That answer, of course, is His forgiveness.

When we confess our wrongdoings and repent, we are forgiven by the One who created us. Genuine repentance requires more than simply offering God apologies for our misdeeds. Real repentance may start with feelings of sorrow and remorse, but it ends only when we turn away from the behaviors that have heretofore distanced us from our Creator. In truth, we offer our most meaningful apologies to God, not with our words, but with our actions. As long as we are still engaged in misbehavior, we may be "repenting," but we have not fully "repented."

Are you troubled by feelings of guilt or regret? If so, you must repent from your mistakes, and you must ask your heavenly Father for His forgiveness. When you do so, He will forgive you completely and without reservation. Then you must forgive yourself just as God has forgiven you: thoroughly, unconditionally, and eternally.

More from God's Word

How can I know all the sins lurking in my heart?
Cleanse me from these hidden faults. Keep your
servant from deliberate sins! Don't let them control me.
Then I will be free of guilt and innocent of great sin.

PSALM 19:12–13 NLT

Be gracious to me, God, according to Your faithful
love; according to Your abundant compassion,
blot out my rebellion. Wash away my guilt,
and cleanse me from my sin.

PSALM 51:1–2 HCSB

Let us come near to God with a sincere heart
and a sure faith, because we have been made
free from a guilty conscience, and our bodies
have been washed with pure water.

HEBREWS 10:22 NCV

Create in me a pure heart, God,
and make my spirit right again.

PSALM 51:10 NCV

Consider my affliction and rescue me,
for I have not forgotten Your instruction.

PSALM 119:153 HCSB

More Thoughts about Guilt

*The redemption, accomplished for us by our Lord
Jesus Christ on the cross at Calvary, is redemption
from the power of sin as well as from its guilt.
Christ is able to save all who come unto God by Him.*

HANNAH WHITALL SMITH

*Guilt is an appalling waste of energy; you can't
build on it. It's only good for wallowing in.*

KATHERINE MANSFIELD

*The most marvelous ingredient in the forgiveness
of God is that He also forgets, the one thing
a human being cannot do. With God, forgetting
is a divine attribute. God's forgiveness forgets.*

OSWALD CHAMBERS

*God's mercy is boundless, free, and, through
Jesus Christ our Lord, available
to us in our present situation.*

A. W. TOZER

*God does not wish us to remember
what He is willing to forget.*

GEORGE A. BUTTRICK

9

The Question

I have so many things to do and so many responsibilities to fulfill, it's hard to make time for God. What does the Bible say about putting God first in my life?

The Answer

God's Word is clear: If you put Him first in every aspect of your life, you'll be blessed. But if you relegate God to a position of lesser importance, you'll suffer the inevitable consequences that result from misplaced priorities.

We live in a hostile world that constantly seeks to pull us away from God.

BILLY GRAHAM

God First

You shall have no other gods before Me.
Exodus 20:3 NKJV

In the twentieth chapter of Exodus, God warns us that we must put Him first, and that we must never place other gods before Him. Yet people who suffer from the ravages of addiction are constantly forced to choose between putting God first or succumbing to the urges that enslave them. More often than not, the urges win, with devastating consequences.

In our busy, complicated world, we are tempted to place our Lord in second, third, or fourth place as we focus on other things. When we place our desires for possessions and status above our love for God—or when we yield to the addictions that threaten to destroy us—we forfeit the peace that might otherwise be ours.

In the wilderness, Satan offered Jesus earthly power and unimaginable riches, but Jesus refused. Instead, He chose to worship His heavenly Father. We must do likewise by putting God first and worshiping Him only. God must come first. Always first.

More from God's Word

*Therefore, whether you eat or drink,
or whatever you do, do all to the glory of God.*
1 Corinthians 10:31 NKJV

*This is the love of God, that we keep
His commandments. And His commandments
are not burdensome.*
1 John 5:3 NKJV

*How happy is everyone who fears the Lord,
who walks in His ways!*
Psalm 128:1 HCSB

*Prove yourselves doers of the word,
and not merely hearers who delude themselves.*
James 1:22 NASB

We love him, because he first loved us.
1 John 4:19 KJV

More Thoughts about Putting God First

Christ is either Lord of all, or He is not Lord at all.
HUDSON TAYLOR

*The most important thing you must decide
to do every day is put the Lord first.*
ELIZABETH GEORGE

*God wants to be in our leisure time as much
as He is in our churches and in our work.*
BETH MOORE

*Even the most routine part of your day
can be a spiritual act of worship.*
SARAH YOUNG

*Jesus Christ is the first and last, author and finisher,
beginning and end, alpha and omega, and by
Him all other things hold together. He must be first
or nothing. God never comes next!*
VANCE HAVNER

10

The Question

Some people tell me that I have a problem,
but I don't think so. Who's right?

The Answer

Denial is a hallmark of addiction.
If other people tell you that you have a problem
with an addictive substance or behavior,
you probably have a problem.

*Our adversary is a master strategist,
forever fogging up our minds with smokescreens.*

CHARLES SWINDOLL

Understanding Denial

*Everyone who practices wicked things hates
the light and avoids it, so that his deeds may
not be exposed. But anyone who lives
by the truth comes to the light, so that his works
may be shown to be accomplished by God.*

JOHN 3:20–21 HCSB

In the field of addiction treatment, the term "denial" refers to a psychological defense mechanism that causes addicts to subconsciously reject reality concerning the use, the abuse, and the consequences of their addictions. As a result of denial, addicts often lack insight into their disease, so they see no need for treatment.

Denial is one of the hallmarks of addiction. In fact, it's one of the key features of the disease; it allows the addict to ignore the warning signs that are patently obvious to family, friends, and complete strangers.

Most addicts steadfastly refuse to admit that they have a problem, at least initially. In its early stages, the addiction may seem to be nothing more than a harmless diversion, a way to reduce stress, to "let off steam," or to "have some fun." With little incentive to change, the addict continues to abuse, thus re-wiring important pathways in the brain, causing permanent changes in neural functioning. Usually it takes a wake-up call of some type, or a catastrophic addiction-related event, to bring the addict to treatment.

The words of John 8:32 are both familiar and profound: "Ye shall know the truth, and the truth shall make you free" (KJV). God is vitally concerned with truth. His Word teaches the truth; His Spirit reveals the truth; His Son leads us to the truth. When we open our hearts to Him, and when we allow His Son to rule over our thoughts and our lives, the Lord reveals Himself, and we come to understand the truth about ourselves and the Truth (with a capital T) about God's gift of grace.

Truth and denial cannot coexist in the same mind. Truth is God's way, and it must be our way, too.

More from God's Word

Learn the truth and never reject it.
Get wisdom, self-control, and understanding.
PROVERBS 23:23 NCV

Be sober, be vigilant; because your adversary
the devil walks about like a roaring lion,
seeking whom he may devour.
1 PETER 5:8 NKJV

Let integrity and uprightness preserve me,
for I wait for You.
PSALM 25:21 NKJV

Teach me Your way, O LORD,
and lead me in a level path.
PSALM 27:11 NASB

You will know the truth,
and the truth will set you free.
JOHN 8:32 HCSB

More Thoughts about Denial

*The devil is the god of this world,
and he has blinded our eyes.*

BILLY GRAHAM

*You and I have need of the strongest spell
that can be found to wake us from
the evil enchantment of worldliness.*

C. S. LEWIS

*Our adversary is a master strategist,
forever fogging up our minds with smokescreens.*

CHARLES SWINDOLL

A fault, once denied, is twice committed.

THOMAS FULLER

If you believe a lie, it will become truth to you.

EDWIN LOUIS COLE

11

The Question

Maybe I have a problem with drugs or alcohol, but it's not my fault. Other people are driving me crazy. It's their fault.

The Answer

When you look in the mirror, you're looking at the person who's responsible for your behavior, your thoughts, and your life. It's a mistake— and it's counterproductive—to blame others for your problems.

Man must cease attributing his problems to his environment, and learn again to exercise his will—his personal responsibility in the realm of faith and morals.

ALBERT SCHWEITZER

Don't Blame Others

It's easy to get "hooked" on feelings of self-righteousness; it's comforting to feel righteous indignation as you blame others for your problems. It's easy to accuse other people of causing your pain. But blame quickly leads to anger, and then to self-justification, both of which are self-destructive.

Douglas Cook, MD

When someone is struggling with addiction, it's easy—almost second nature—to blame others for the troubles that inevitably spring up as the illness takes its toll. Playing the blame game is easy, but it's wrong.

Whenever we blame others for our own problems, we waste both time and energy. Yet blaming seems to be a favorite human pastime. Why? Because blaming is much easier than fixing. So instead of solving our problems legitimately (by doing the hard work required to solve them) we're inclined to blame, to complain, to criticize, and to do precious little else. Meanwhile, the problems we've created remain unsolved.

So if you find yourself playing the blame game, quit playing. Instead of looking for someone to blame, look for something to fix, and then get busy fixing it. And as you consider your own situation, remember this: God has a way of helping those who help themselves, but He doesn't spend much time helping those who don't.

More from God's Word

*All bitterness, anger and wrath, shouting
and slander must be removed from you,
along with all malice. And be kind and
compassionate to one another, forgiving
one another, just as God also forgave you in Christ.*
EPHESIANS 4:31–32 HCSB

*Each person should examine his own work,
and then he will have a reason for boasting in
himself alone, and not in respect to someone else.
For each person will have to carry his own load.*
GALATIANS 6:4–5 HCSB

*Don't let your spirit rush to be angry,
for anger abides in the heart of fools.*
ECCLESIASTES 7:9 HCSB

*Therefore, laying aside falsehood,
speak truth each one of you with his neighbor,
for we are members of one another.*
EPHESIANS 4:25 NASB

*The heart knows its own bitterness,
and a stranger does not share its joy.*
PROVERBS 14:10 NKJV

More Thoughts about Blame

Bear with the faults of others
as you would have them bear with yours.

PHILLIPS BROOKS

Make no excuses. Rationalize nothing.
Blame no one. Humble yourself.

BETH MOORE

Do not think of the faults of others
but what is good in them and faulty in yourself.

ST. TERESA OF AVILA

The fault, dear Brutus, is not in our stars,
but in ourselves.

WILLIAM SHAKESPEARE

You'll never win the blame game,
so why even bother to play?

MARIE T. FREEMAN

12

The Question

I think I might have a problem with addiction,
but I don't know where to go for help.
What should I do?

The Answer

Help is readily available, and you can start
in many different ways. Thankfully, in today's
addictive society, treatment options are plentiful.

—⟋⟍—

*Addiction is considered a highly treatable
disease, and recovery is attainable. Currently,
about 10 percent of American adults, age
eighteen or older, claim to be in recovery
from an alcohol or drug abuse issue.*

THE NEW YORK STATE OFFICE ON ALCOHOLISM
AND SUBSTANCE ABUSE SERVICES

Help Is Always Available

If you have a problem with alcohol, does that mean that you are a weak person? Absolutely not. It means that you have developed a disease.

Douglas Cook, MD

If you have an addiction, and if you decide to seek treatment, you won't have to look very far. A wide range of treatment options are readily available, and some of them are free. Alcoholics Anonymous, for example, costs nothing and has helped millions of alcoholics gain sobriety. Other twelve-step programs, such as Narcotics Anonymous, are not-for-profit fellowships that welcome addicts from every walk of life.

If twelve-step programs don't seem right for you, other options include individual counseling, outpatient treatment, and inpatient treatment. And you should also schedule a visit with your primary care physician for a regular checkup. So if you're concerned about your own addiction, or if someone you trust has suggested that you need help, don't worry and don't delay. There's a treatment option out there that's right for you.

More from God's Word

*Peace, peace to you, and peace
to him who helps you, for your God helps you.*
1 Chronicles 12:18 HCSB

*The Lord is my strength and my song;
He has become my salvation.*
Exodus 15:2 HCSB

*For I, Yahweh your God, hold your right hand and
say to you: Do not fear, I will help you.*
Isaiah 41:13 HCSB

Wait on the Lord, and He will rescue you.
Proverbs 20:22 HCSB

*We can be sure when we say,
"I will not be afraid, because the Lord is my helper.
People can't do anything to me."*
Hebrews 13:6 NCV

Risk Factors for Addiction

People of any age or economic status can become addicted to a drug. However, certain factors can affect the likelihood and speed of developing an addiction:

- Family history of addiction. Drug addiction is more common in some families and likely involves genetic predisposition. If you have a blood relative, such as a parent or sibling, with alcohol or drug problems, you're at greater risk of developing a drug addiction.

- Being male. Men are more likely to have problems with drugs than women are. However, progression of addictive disorders is known to be faster in females.

- Having another mental health disorder. If you have a mental health disorder such as depression, attention-deficit/hyperactivity disorder (ADHD), or post-traumatic stress disorder, you're more likely to become dependent on drugs.

- Peer pressure. Peer pressure is a strong factor in starting to use and abuse drugs, particularly for young people.

- Lack of family involvement. Difficult family situations or lack of a bond with your parents or siblings may increase the risk of addiction, as can a lack of parental supervision.

- Anxiety, depression, and loneliness. Using drugs can become a way of coping with these painful psychological feelings and can make these problems even worse.

- Taking a highly addictive drug. Some drugs, such as stimulants, cocaine, or painkillers, may result in faster development of addiction than other drugs. However, taking drugs considered less addicting—so-called "light drugs"—can start you on a pathway of drug use and addiction.

SOURCE: MAYO CLINIC

13

The Question

I don't trust doctors; I don't think treatment centers work; and I don't want to go to twelve-step meetings. Do these things actually work?

The Answer

No single treatment method works for all addicts, but treatment methods are effective. And twelve-step programs have helped millions of addicts gain and maintain sobriety.

Addiction doesn't happen overnight.
It's a gradual progression—
and so is the treatment and recovery process.

HAZELDEN BETTY FORD FOUNDATION

Treatment Options

*People who have never had an addiction
don't understand how hard it can be.*

PAYNE STEWART

Addiction is a complex disease that can disrupt families and destroy lives. Thankfully, a wide range of treatment options are available. Treatment can be as straightforward as attending a local twelve-step program. Other options include outpatient programs, one-on-one counseling, inpatient programs, and hospitalization.

Drug addiction can be treated, but the healing process is not simple. Because addiction is a chronic disease, people can't simply stop using drugs for a few days and be cured. Most patients need long-term or repeated care to remain sober and recover their lives.

Successful treatment has several steps:

- detoxification (the process by which the body rids itself of a drug)
- behavioral counseling
- medication (for opioid, tobacco, or alcohol addiction)
- evaluation and treatment for co-occurring mental health issues such as depression and anxiety
- long-term follow-up to prevent relapse

A range of care with a tailored treatment program and follow-up options can be crucial to success. Treatment should include both medical and mental health services as needed. Follow-up care may include community- or family-based recovery support systems.

NATIONAL INSTITUTE OF DRUG ABUSE

More from God's Word

The wisdom that is from above is first pure,
then peaceable, gentle, willing to yield,
full of mercy and good fruits,
without partiality and without hypocrisy.
JAMES 3:17 NKJV

He that walketh with wise men shall be wise:
but a companion of fools shall be destroyed.
PROVERBS 13:20 KJV

If any of you lacks wisdom, let him ask of God,
who gives to all generously and without reproach,
and it will be given to him.
JAMES 1:5 NASB

Who among you is wise and understanding?
Let him show by his good behavior his deeds
in the gentleness of wisdom.
JAMES 3:13 NASB

Get wisdom—how much better it is than gold!
And get understanding—it is preferable to silver.
PROVERBS 16:16 HCSB

More Thoughts about Treatment

Over 115,000 Alcoholics Anonymous (AA) groups exist in more than 175 countries around the world, serving more than 2 million members.

There continues to be a large "treatment gap" in this country. In a recent survey, an estimated 22.7 million Americans (8.6 percent) needed treatment for a problem related to drugs or alcohol, but only about 2.5 million people (0.9 percent) received treatment at a specialty facility.

NATIONAL INSTITUTE ON DRUG ABUSE

Breaking an addiction usually requires changes in many different areas of life.

GERALD MAY, MD

14

The Question

Sometimes it feels like there's no hope for me.
What should I do?

The Answer

Never abandon hope. Keep praying;
get treatment; repeat.

*There is hope for the alcoholic.
God is able to deliver from this
as well as any other addiction.*

BILLY GRAHAM

Never Abandon Hope

Let us hold fast the confession of our hope without wavering, for He who promised is faithful.

HEBREWS 10:23 NASB

God's promises give us hope: hope for today, hope for tomorrow, and hope for all eternity. The hope that the world offers is temporary, at best. But the hope that God offers never grows old and never goes out of date. It's no wonder, then, that when we pin our hopes on worldly resources, we are often disappointed. Thankfully, God has no such record of failure.

The disease of addiction robs us of hope. But the Bible teaches that the Lord blesses those who trust in His wisdom and follow in the footsteps of His Son. Will you count yourself among that number? When you do, you'll have every reason on earth—and in heaven—to be hopeful about your future. After all, God has made important promises to you, promises that He is certainly going to keep. So be hopeful, be optimistic, be faithful, and adhere to your treatment regimen one day at a time. Then leave the rest up to God. Your destiny is safe with Him.

More from God's Word

I say to myself, "The LORD is mine, so I hope in him."
LAMENTATIONS 3:24 NCV

Be strong and courageous,
all you who put your hope in the LORD.
PSALM 31:24 HCSB

Hope deferred makes the heart sick.
PROVERBS 13:12 NKJV

This hope we have as an anchor of the soul,
a hope both sure and steadfast.
HEBREWS 6:19 NASB

The LORD is good to those who wait for Him,
to the soul who seeks Him. It is good
that one should hope and wait quietly
for the salvation of the LORD.
LAMENTATIONS 3:25–26 NKJV

More Thoughts about Hope

*If your hopes are being disappointed just now,
it means that they are being purified.*

OSWALD CHAMBERS

*The presence of hope in the invincible
sovereignty of God drives out fear.*

JOHN PIPER

*The earth's troubles fade
in the light of heaven's hope.*

BILLY GRAHAM

*Jesus gives us hope because He keeps
us company, has a vision, and knows
the way we should go.*

MAX LUCADO

*God is the only one who can make
the valley of trouble a door of hope.*

CATHERINE MARSHALL

15

The Question

Once I stop using the addictive substance,
what's the danger of relapse?

The Answer

Similar to other chronic, relapsing diseases
such as diabetes, asthma, and heart disease,
drug addiction can be managed successfully.
And as with other chronic diseases, it is not
uncommon for a person to relapse and begin
abusing drugs again. Relapse, however, does not
signal treatment failure—rather, it indicates that
treatment should be reinstated or adjusted or that
an alternative treatment is needed to help the
individual regain control and recover.

NATIONAL COUNCIL ON ALCOHOL AND DRUG DEPENDENCE

*You can be sure that Satan will tempt you
at your weak point, not the strong.*

BILLY GRAHAM

Understanding Relapse

We are hard-pressed on every side, yet not crushed; we are perplexed, but not in despair.

2 CORINTHIANS 4:8 NKJV

Addiction is a chronic illness, which means that addicts are not cured "once and for all." The possibility of relapse is part of the disease. In fact, many, if not most, people who enter treatment will experience at least one relapse. A relapse doesn't mean that the patient is doomed or that sobriety is impossible. On the contrary, a relapse can become an important part of the recovery process if the addict reenters treatment and learns something from the experience.

A relapse is a call to action and, like any medical emergency, it requires immediate attention in order to rectify the behavior and avoid repeating it.

The longer the relapse, the more problems it creates for the addict. So any day is a good day to pick up the broken pieces and begin to put a recovery program back together. And with God's help, it's always possible for an addict to regain sobriety and return to treatment. In fact, it happens every day.

More from God's Word

I called to the LORD in my distress; I called
to my God. From His temple He heard my voice.
2 SAMUEL 22:7 HCSB

The LORD is my rock, my fortress, and my deliverer,
my God, my mountain where I seek refuge.
My shield, the horn of my salvation,
my stronghold, my refuge, and my Savior.
2 SAMUEL 22:2–3 HCSB

God blesses those who patiently endure
testing and temptation. Afterward they
will receive the crown of life that
God has promised to those who love him.
JAMES 1:12 NLT

He heals the brokenhearted
and binds up their wounds.
PSALM 147:3 HCSB

The LORD is my shepherd; I shall not want.
PSALM 23:1 KJV

More Thoughts about Relapse

Like other chronic diseases, addiction often involves cycles of relapse and remission. Without treatment or engagement in recovery activities, addiction is progressive and can result in disability or premature death.

AMERICAN SOCIETY OF ADDICTION MEDICINE

Relapse rates while patients are in treatment are approximately 40 percent to 60 percent.

NATIONAL INSTITUTE OF DRUG ABUSE

What Causes a Relapse?

Unfortunately, relapse after a period of sobriety is a common occurrence. Signs of an approaching relapse include the following:
- not making sobriety your top priority
- not having a support system
- not wanting to quit for yourself
- not being prepared for life post-treatment

After a relapse, many people experience feelings of shame or regret. You may feel like giving up the fight and giving in to your addiction rather than continuing to work hard and overcome the fleeting desire to use.

Instead, use this relapse as a learning tool; clarify your relapse prevention plan and identify your triggers. By digging deeper into the root cause of the relapse, you will lay the foundation for a recovery that will ensure you bounce back stronger than ever.

ADDICTIONCENTER.COM

16

The Question

I've tried just about everything I can think of to overcome my addiction, but nothing seems to work. I feel like giving up. What should I do?

The Answer

If the first treatment you try doesn't work as quickly or as well as you'd like, don't give up. With the miraculous tools of modern medicine, and with God's help, you will eventually find a treatment that works for you if you keep trying.

*The marathons—the relentless,
continual tests that won't go away—
these are the ones that bruise but build character.*

CHARLES SWINDOLL

Don't Give Up

Let us not become weary in doing good,
for at the proper time we will reap
a harvest if we do not give up.

GALATIANS 6:9 NIV

Recovering from any addiction requires determination and perseverance because the road to recovery is often a long and twisting path. Calvin Coolidge observed, "Nothing in the world can take the place of persistence. Talent will not; genius will not; education will not. Persistence and determination alone are omnipotent." President Coolidge was right. Perseverance pays.

The Bible teaches us to persevere: "You need endurance, so that after you have done God's will, you may receive what was promised." These reassuring words from Hebrews 10:36 (HCSB) remind us that if we refuse to give up, we will eventually receive that which God has promised. Even when we fail, God is faithful. When we stumble, He picks us up and encourages us to try again. What's required of us is perseverance, not perfection.

If you're determined to recover from your addiction, God stands ready to help you meet that challenge. And while you're waiting for His plans to unfold, you can be comforted in the knowledge that your Creator can overcome any obstacle, even if you cannot.

More from God's Word

We are hard-pressed on every side, yet not crushed; we are perplexed, but not in despair.
2 CORINTHIANS 4:8 NKJV

Let us run the race that is before us and never give up. We should remove from our lives anything that would get in the way and the sin that so easily holds us back.
HEBREWS 12:1 NCV

You have need of endurance, so that when you have done the will of God, you may receive what was promised.
HEBREWS 10:36 NASB

As for you, be strong; don't be discouraged, for your work has a reward.
2 CHRONICLES 15:7 HCSB

Finishing is better than starting. Patience is better than pride.
ECCLESIASTES 7:8 NLT

More Thoughts about Perseverance

*Success or failure can be pretty well predicted
by the degree to which the heart is fully in it.*

JOHN ELDREDGE

*Perseverance is more than endurance.
It is endurance combined with absolute
assurance and certainty that what
we are looking for is going to happen.*

OSWALD CHAMBERS

*Patience and diligence,
like faith, remove mountains.*

WILLIAM PENN

*Everyone gets discouraged. The question is:
Are you going to give up or get up? It's a choice.*

JOHN MAXWELL

*Perseverance is not a passive submission
to circumstances—it is a strong and active
response to the difficult events of life.*

ELIZABETH GEORGE

17

The Question

The world's value system glorifies partying.
But that's the very thing I'm trying to escape from.
What should I do?

The Answer

God's Word teaches us to pay less attention
to the world and more attention to Him.
The world is filled with distractions and
temptations. So we must focus on Him.

*For Christ, the way to abundant grace
and forgiveness is through Himself, away
from all possible objects of attachment.*

GERALD MAY, MD

Less Attachment
to the World

*Do not be conformed to this world,
but be transformed by the renewing of your mind,
that you may prove what is that good
and acceptable and perfect will of God.*

Romans 12:2 NKJV

We live in this world, but we should not worship it. Yet we are bombarded by messages and distractions that tempt us to do otherwise. The twenty-first-century world in which we live is a noisy, confusing place. The world seems to cry, "Worship me with your money, your time, your energy, your thoughts, and your life." But if we are wise, we won't worship the world; we will worship God.

You must distance yourself from the temptations and distractions of modern-day society. But distancing yourself isn't easy, especially when so many societal forces are struggling to capture your attention, your participation, and your money.

All of mankind is engaged in a colossal, worldwide treasure hunt. Some people seek treasure from earthly sources; others seek God's treasures by making Him the cornerstone of their lives. What kind of treasure hunter are you? Are you so caught up in the demands of everyday living that you sometimes allow the search for worldly treasures to become your primary focus? If so, it's time to reorganize your daily to-do list by placing God in His rightful place: first place. Don't allow anyone or anything to separate you from your heavenly Father and His only begotten Son.

More from God's Word

*No one can serve two masters. For you will hate
one and love the other; you will be devoted
to one and despise the other. You cannot
serve God and be enslaved to money.*

LUKE 16:13 NLT

*Pure and undefiled religion before our God
and Father is this: to look after orphans and widows
in their distress and to keep oneself unstained
by the world.*

JAMES 1:27 HCSB

*Set your mind on the things above,
not on the things that are on earth.*

COLOSSIANS 3:2 NASB

*Our citizenship is in heaven, from which also
we eagerly wait for a Savior, the Lord Jesus Christ.*

PHILIPPIANS 3:20 NASB

*Don't you know that friendship with the world
is hostility toward God? So whoever wants
to be the world's friend becomes God's enemy.*

JAMES 4:4 HCSB

More Thoughts about Worldliness

*We need more love for the Word
and less love for the world.*

R. G. LEE

*The voices of the world are a cacophony
of chaos, pulling you this way and that.
Don't listen to those voices.*

SARAH YOUNG

*Worldliness is an inner attitude that puts self
at the center of life instead of God.*

BILLY GRAHAM

*Loving the world destroys our relationship
with God, it denies our faith in God,
and it discounts our future with God.*

DAVID JEREMIAH

*We live in a hostile world that constantly seeks
to pull us away from God.*

BILLY GRAHAM

18

The Question

What does the Bible say about prayer?

The Answer

God's Word teaches us that prayer
is an essential part of a well-lived life.
One way to make sure that your heart
is in tune with God is to pray often.
The more you talk to Him,
the more He will talk to you.

*If you believe, you will receive
whatever you ask for in prayer.*
MATTHEW 21:22 HCSB

The Power of Prayer

Rejoice always, pray without ceasing,
in everything give thanks;
for this is the will of God in Christ Jesus for you.
1 THESSALONIANS 5:16–18 NKJV

If you're attempting to overcome an addiction, prayer can be a powerful tool that you can use to change your world and change yourself. God hears every prayer and responds in His own way and according to His own timetable. When you make a habit of consulting Him about everything, He'll guide you along the path of His choosing, which, by the way, is the path you should take.

When you petition the Lord for strength, He'll give you the courage to face your addiction, the courage to seek treatment, and the strength to stay in treatment. So today, instead of turning things over in your mind, turn them over to God in prayer. Take your concerns to the Lord and leave them there. Your heavenly Father is listening, and He wants to hear from you. Now.

More from God's Word

Is anyone among you suffering? He should pray.
JAMES 5:13 HCSB

Ask and it will be given to you; seek and you will find; knock and it will be opened to you. For every one who asks receives, and he who seeks finds, and to him who knocks it will be opened.
MATTHEW 7:7–8 NASB

Whenever you stand praying, if you have anything against anyone, forgive him, so that your Father in heaven may also forgive you your wrongdoing.
MARK 11:25 HCSB

I desire therefore that the men pray everywhere, lifting up holy hands, without wrath and doubting.
1 TIMOTHY 2:8 NKJV

Confess your trespasses to one another, and pray for one another, that you may be healed. The effective, fervent prayer of a righteous man avails much.

JAMES 5:16 NKJV

More Thoughts about Prayer

*It is impossible to overstate the need
for prayer in the fabric of family life.*

JAMES DOBSON

Prayer is our lifeline to God.

BILLY GRAHAM

*Don't pray when you feel like it. Have an
appointment with the Lord and keep it.*

CORRIE TEN BOOM

*Two wings are necessary to lift our souls
toward God: prayer and praise.
Prayer asks. Praise accepts the answer.*

LETTIE COWMAN

*Any concern that is too small to be turned into
a prayer is too small to be made into a burden.*

CORRIE TEN BOOM

19

The Question

I can't always find time to study my Bible
every day. What does the Bible
say about my daily devotions?

The Answer

Your Creator wants you to get reacquainted
with His Word every day. Would you like
a foolproof formula for a better life?
Here it is: Stay in close contact with God.

*Truly my soul silently waits for God;
from Him comes my salvation.*
PSALM 62:1 NKJV

The Daily Devotional

*Morning by morning he wakens me and opens
my understanding to his will. The Sovereign Lord
has spoken to me, and I have listened.*

Isaiah 50:4–5 NLT

As you overcome your addiction day by day, it pays to spend
time with God day by day.

Every new day is a gift from the Creator, a gift that allows
each of us to say "thank You" by spending time with the Giver.
When we begin the day with our Bibles open and our hearts
attuned to God, we are inevitably blessed by the promises we
find in His Word. During the quiet moments we spend with
the Lord, He guides us, He leads us, and He touches our hearts.

Each day of your life has 1,440 minutes, and God deserves
a few of them. And you deserve the experience of spending a few
quiet minutes every morning with your Creator.

So if you haven't already done so, establish the habit of
spending time with the Lord every day of the week. It's a habit
that will change your day and revolutionize your life. When you
give the Lord your undivided attention, everything changes,
including you.

More from God's Word

Heaven and earth will pass away,
but My words will never pass away.
MATTHEW 24:35 HCSB

Grow in the grace and knowledge of our Lord
and Savior Jesus Christ. To Him be the glory
both now and to the day of eternity.
2 PETER 3:18 HCSB

Early the next morning, while it was still dark,
Jesus woke and left the house.
He went to a lonely place, where he prayed.
MARK 1:35 NCV

It is good to give thanks to the LORD,
and to sing praises to Your name, O Most High.
PSALM 92:1 NKJV

Thy word is a lamp unto my feet,
and a light unto my path.
PSALM 119:105 KJV

More Thoughts about Your Daily Devotional

Doesn't God deserve the best minutes of your day?
BILLY GRAHAM

*Make it the first morning business of your life
to understand some part of the Bible clearly,
and make it your daily business to obey it.*
JOHN RUSKIN

*Begin each day with God.
It will change your priorities.*
ELIZABETH GEORGE

*Relying on God has to begin all over again
every day as if nothing had yet been done.*
C. S. LEWIS

*Whatever is your best time in the day,
give that to communion with God.*
HUDSON TAYLOR

20

The Question

I feel like giving up. What can I do?

The Answer

When you feel that all hope is gone, turn to God.
His power is limitless, as is His love.

—⊪—

There is no limit to God.
There is no limit to His power.
There is no limit to His love.
There is no limit to His mercy.

BILLY GRAHAM

God: Your Higher Power

*His divine power has given us everything we need
for a godly life through our knowledge of him who
called us by his own glory and goodness.*

2 PETER 1:3 NIV

God's Word promises that He will support you in good times and comfort you in hard times. The Creator of the universe stands ready to give you the strength to meet any challenge, including the challenge of addiction. When you ask for God's help, He responds in His own way and at His own appointed hour. But make no mistake: He always responds.

In a world brimming with life-threatening addictions, God's grace is the ultimate armor. In a world saturated with misleading messages, God's Word is the ultimate truth. In a world filled with frustrations and distractions, God's Son offers the ultimate peace.

Today, as you encounter the inevitable challenges of twenty-first-century life, remember that your heavenly Father never leaves you, not even for a moment. He's always available, always ready to listen, always ready to lead. When you make a habit of talking to Him early and often, His power will keep you safe, now and forever.

More from God's Word

Is anything impossible for the Lord?
GENESIS 18:14 HCSB

You are the God of great wonders!
You demonstrate your awesome power
among the nations.
PSALM 77:14 NLT

Depend on the Lord and his strength; always go
to him for help. Remember the miracles he has
done; remember his wonders and his decisions.
PSALM 105:4–5 NCV

The Lord your God is the God of gods and Lord
of lords, the great, mighty, and awesome God.
DEUTERONOMY 10:17 HCSB

Jesus looked at them and said, "With men this
is impossible, but with God all things are possible."
MATTHEW 19:26 HCSB

More Thoughts
about God's Power

*God's specialty is raising dead things to life
and making impossible things possible. You don't
have the need that exceeds His power.*

BETH MOORE

*Of course you will encounter trouble.
But behold a God of power who can take
any evil and turn it into a door of hope.*

CATHERINE MARSHALL

*To yield to God means to belong to God,
and to belong to God means to have all His infinite
power. To belong to God means to have all.*

HANNAH WHITALL SMITH

God is able to do what we can't do.

BILLY GRAHAM

Kept by His power—that is the only safety.

OSWALD CHAMBERS

21

The Question

My pain is intense, and sometimes it seems like I'll never recover. Is it possible for me to heal?

The Answer

With God all things are possible.
And with the miracles of modern medicine, depression is highly treatable. So pray to your Creator and consult with your physician. When you do, help is on the way. Soon.

*If all things are possible with God,
then all things are possible
to him who believes in Him.*

CORRIE TEN BOOM

With God All Things Are Possible

Jesus looked at them and said to them,
"With men this is impossible,
but with God all things are possible."

MATTHEW 19:26 NKJV

If you've struggled with addiction, you may have wondered if recovery is possible. If so, wonder no more. With God all things are possible. With proper treatment, and with God's help, you can overcome your illness and remain addiction free.

God has put you in a particular place, and at a specific time, of His choosing. He has an assignment that is uniquely yours, tasks that are specially intended just for you. And whether you know it or not, He's equipped you with everything you need to fulfill His purpose and achieve His plans.

The next time you find yourself fretting about the future or worrying about the challenge of treating a chronic illness, refocus your thoughts on the positive aspects of life here on earth and life eternal in heaven. And while you're at it, remember that God will guide your steps if you let Him. When you allow the Lord to take over, there's simply no limit to the things that the two of you, working together, can accomplish.

More from God's Word

*Jesus said to him, "If you can believe,
all things are possible to him who believes."*
MARK 9:23 NKJV

Is anything too hard for the LORD?
GENESIS 18:14 KJV

*Therefore we do not lose heart. Even though
our outward man is perishing, yet the inward
man is being renewed day by day.*
2 CORINTHIANS 4:16 NKJV

*I can do all things through Christ
which strengtheneth me.*
PHILIPPIANS 4:13 KJV

*The things which are impossible
with men are possible with God.*
LUKE 18:27 KJV

More Thoughts about Possibilities

*We are all faced with a series of great opportunities
brilliantly disguised as impossible situations.*

CHARLES SWINDOLL

*Do not limit the limitless God! With Him, face
the future unafraid because you are never alone.*

LETTIE COWMAN

*Alleged "impossibilities" are opportunities
for our capacities to be stretched.*

CHARLES SWINDOLL

A possibility is a hint from God.

SØREN KIERKEGAARD

*I have found that there are three stages in every
great work of God: first, it is impossible,
then it is difficult, then it is done.*

HUDSON TAYLOR

22

The Question

Sometimes it's hard to be patient, especially when I'm so impatient to somehow conquer my addiction. What advice can I find in God's Word?

The Answer

The Bible teaches us that patience is better than strength. When dealing with the illness of addiction, staying sober is a marathon, not a sprint.

Patience and diligence, like faith, move mountains.

WILLIAM PENN

Be Patient

Better to be patient than powerful;
better to have self-control than to conquer a city.
PROVERBS 16:32 NLT

Perhaps you're waiting to get into treatment. Or maybe you're praying for a loved one who's still engaging in addictive behavior. Either way, you need patience. Proverbs 16:32 teaches, "Better to be patient than powerful; better to have self-control than to conquer a city" (NLT). But for most of us, patience is difficult. We know precisely what we want, and we know precisely when we want it: now. Yet the Lord instructs us to be patient. As believers, we must strive to obey Him, even when it's hard.

Our heavenly Father, in His infinite wisdom, operates according to His own timetable, not ours. He has plans that we cannot see and purposes we cannot know. He has created a world that unfolds according to His schedule, not ours.

So if you've been waiting impatiently for the Lord to answer your prayers, it's time to put a stop to all that needless worry. You can be sure that God will answer your prayers when He knows the time is right. Your job is to keep praying—and working—until He does.

More from God's Word

A man's wisdom gives him patience;
it is to his glory to overlook an offense.
PROVERBS 19:11 NIV

The LORD is good to those who depend on him,
to those who search for him. So it is good to wait
quietly for salvation from the LORD.
LAMENTATIONS 3:25–26 NLT

Be joyful in hope,
patient in affliction,
faithful in prayer.
ROMANS 12:12 NIV

Patience of spirit is better than haughtiness of spirit.
ECCLESIASTES 7:8 NASB

If we hope for what we do not yet have,
we wait for it patiently.
ROMANS 8:25 NIV

More Thoughts about Patience

Frustration is not the will of God.
There is time to do anything
and everything that God wants us to do.
ELISABETH ELLIOT

Patience is the companion of wisdom.
ST. AUGUSTINE

Today, take a complicated situation
and with time, patience, and a smile,
turn it into something positive—
for you and for others.
JONI EARECKSON TADA

Patience graciously, compassionately,
and with understanding judges the faults
of others without unjust criticism.
BILLY GRAHAM

Teach us, O Lord, the disciplines of patience,
for to wait is often harder than to work.
PETER MARSHALL

23

The Question

A loved one needs help, and I'm convinced the problem is addiction. We've talked about it at length, but nothing seems to help. What else can I do?

The Answer

If you believe the situation is serious enough, you may want to consider enlisting other concerned family members to help you stage an intervention.

—⁂—

He climbs highest who helps another up.

Zig Ziglar

Helping a Loved One by Staging an Intervention

Carry one another's burdens;
in this way you will fulfill the law of Christ.
GALATIANS 6:2 HCSB

If you have a loved one who's struggling with addiction, you already know how painful the disease can be. And you may have learned how difficult it can be to encourage the addict to seek treatment. People struggling with addiction usually deny they have a problem and are reluctant to accept help. An intervention presents a loved one with a structured setting where reality can be discussed and treatment alternatives can be considered. The object, of course, is to help the addict make changes before his or her life spins further out of control.

An intervention should be carefully planned and should be done by family and friends in consultation with a doctor, or with an experienced drug and alcohol counselor, or as directed by an intervention professional. Participants may include family and friends, clergy, or coworkers. During the intervention, these people gather together to have a direct, honest, heart-to-heart conversation with the addict. The ultimate goal of such an intervention is to convince the addict to seek immediate treatment.

Perhaps you feel that an intervention on behalf of your loved one would be a waste of time. If so, it's worth remembering that, with God, all things are possible. So pray about it with an open mind and seek professional guidance. An intervention may be the best way to encourage your loved one to regain a sense of reality and thus see the need for healing.

MAYO CLINIC

More from God's Word

Whenever you are able,
do good to people who need help.
PROVERBS 3:27 NCV

Therefore, as we have opportunity,
we must work for the good of all, especially
for those who belong to the household of faith.
GALATIANS 6:10 HCSB

Whatever you did for one of the least
of these brothers of Mine, you did for Me.
MATTHEW 25:40 HCSB

Let us not become weary in doing good,
for at the proper time we will reap a harvest
if we do not give up.
GALATIANS 6:9 NIV

If you have two shirts, give one to the poor. If you
have food, share it with those who are hungry.
LUKE 3:11 NLT

Recognizing Drug Abuse
in Family Members

Sometimes it's difficult to distinguish normal moodiness or angst from signs of drug use. Possible indications that your teenager or other family member is using drugs include the following:

Problems at school or work—frequently missing school or work, a sudden disinterest in school activities or work, or a drop in grades or work performance

Physical health issues—lack of energy and motivation

Neglected appearance—lack of interest in clothing, grooming, or looks

Changes in behavior—exaggerated efforts to bar family members from entering his or her room, being secretive about where he or she goes with friends, or drastic changes in behavior and relationships with family and friends

Spending money—sudden requests for money without a reasonable explanation; or your discovery that money is missing or has been stolen or that items have disappeared from your home, indicating maybe they're being sold to support drug use

Mayo Clinic

24

The Question

I want to sense God's presence and His love, but it's not easy for me. What should I do?

The Answer

First, remember that God isn't far away. He's right here, right now, and He's ready to talk to you right here, right now. So find a quiet place and open your heart to Him. When you do, you'll sense God's presence and His love, which, by the way, is already surrounding you and your loved ones.

God knows what each one of us is dealing with. He knows our pressures. He knows our conflicts. And He has made a provision for each and every one of them.

KAY ARTHUR

God's Love Never Ends

*The LORD's lovingkindnesses indeed never cease,
for His compassions never fail. They are new
every morning. Great is Your faithfulness.*
LAMENTATIONS 3:22–23 NASB

St. Augustine observed, "God loves each of us as if there were only one of us." Do you believe these words? Do you seek to have an intimate, one-on-one relationship with your heavenly Father, or are you satisfied to keep Him at a "safe" distance?

Sometimes, in the crush of our daily duties, God may seem far away, but He is not. God is everywhere we have ever been and everywhere we will ever go. He is with us night and day; He knows our thoughts and our prayers. And when we earnestly seek Him, we will find Him because He is here, waiting patiently for us to reach out to Him.

Today and every day, remember that God's love endures forever, that His love for you is perfect, and that His love is intended for you. Always.

More from God's Word

He is gracious and compassionate,
slow to anger, rich in faithful love.
JOEL 2:13 HCSB

We have known and believed the love that God
has for us. God is love, and he who abides in love
abides in God, and God in him.
1 JOHN 4:16 NKJV

Give thanks to Him and praise His name.
For Yahweh is good, and His love is eternal;
His faithfulness endures through all generations.
PSALM 100:4–5 HCSB

We love him, because he first loved us.
1 JOHN 4:19 KJV

For God so loved the world, that he gave his only
begotten Son, that whosoever believeth in him
should not perish, but have everlasting life.
JOHN 3:16 KJV

More Thoughts
about God's Love

*God loves you and wants you to experience
peace and life—abundant and eternal.*

Billy Graham

*Even when our choices are destructive
and their consequences hurtful,
God's love remains unwavering.*

Gerald May, MD

*God is the giver, and we are the receivers.
And His richest gifts are bestowed not upon those
who do the greatest things, but upon those
who accept His abundance and His grace.*

Hannah Whitall Smith

*God knows everything. He can manage
everything, and He loves us. Surely this is enough
for a fullness of joy that is beyond words.*

Hannah Whitall Smith

*We do not need to beg Him to bless us;
He simply cannot help it.*

Hannah Whitall Smith

25

The Question

People tell me, "Once an addict, always an addict." That means total abstinence, and I'm having trouble accepting that fact.

The Answer

As you come to grips with your addiction, you'll need to accept the fact that total abstinence is the best way—indeed the only way—to gain and retain sobriety.

Subdue your heart to match your circumstances.

JONI EARECKSON TADA

Accepting Your Addiction

Accept each day as it comes to you.
Do not waste your time and energy
wishing for a different set of circumstances.

SARAH YOUNG

If you're recovering from an addiction, you've probably been told that total abstinence is the only way to remain addiction free. And you may have been quite disturbed by that fact. Nonetheless, you must accept the reality of your addiction—and the need for total abstinence—if you wish to maintain your sobriety.

Reinhold Niebuhr penned a simple verse that has come to be known as the Serenity Prayer. It begins with a simple yet profound request: "God, grant me the serenity to accept the things I cannot change." Niebuhr's words are far easier to recite than they are to live by. Why? Because most of us want life to unfold in accordance with our own wishes. But sometimes God has other plans.

Today, accept the fact that, as a recovering addict, there are some things you simply cannot do. Accept the limitations imposed by your addiction and trust God. When you do, you can be comforted in the knowledge that your Creator is good, that His love endures forever, and that He understands His plans perfectly, even when you do not.

More from God's Word

Should we accept only good things from
the hand of God and never anything bad?
JOB 2:10 NLT

Trust in the LORD with all your heart
and lean not on your own understanding.
PROVERBS 3:5 NIV

Everything God made is good, and nothing
should be refused if it is accepted with thanks.
1 TIMOTHY 4:4 NCV

Now we see in a mirror, dimly,
but then face to face. Now I know in part,
but then I shall know just as I also am known.
1 CORINTHIANS 13:12 NKJV

He is the LORD. He will do what He thinks is good.
1 SAMUEL 3:18 HCSB

More Thoughts
about Acceptance

Christians who are strong in the faith grow as they accept whatever God allows to enter their lives.

BILLY GRAHAM

One of the marks of spiritual maturity is the quiet confidence that God is in control, without the need to understand why He does what He does.

CHARLES SWINDOLL

Loving Him means the thankful acceptance of all things that His love has appointed.

ELISABETH ELLIOT

Acceptance says, "True, this is my situation at the moment. I'll look unblinkingly at the reality of it. But, I'll also open my hands to accept willingly whatever a loving Father sends."

CATHERINE MARSHALL

26

The Question

Why is it important for me to overcome feelings of bitterness?

The Answer

Until you can forgive others and forgive yourself, you'll be trapped in an emotional prison of your own making. Because bitterness is counterproductive to your emotional health, it poses a threat to your sobriety.

—⁓—

Resentment always hurts you
more than the person you resent.
RICK WARREN

Bitterness:
Beware of the Poison

He who says he is in the light, and hates his brother,
is in darkness until now.
1 JOHN 2:9 NKJV

Addiction leads to bitterness, and bitterness is a spiritual sickness. It will consume your soul. It is dangerous to your emotional health, and it can destroy you if you let it.

The world holds few if any rewards for those who remain angrily focused on the past. Still, the act of forgiveness is difficult for all but the most saintly men and women. Being frail, fallible, imperfect human beings, most of us are quick to anger, quick to blame, slow to forgive, and even slower to forget. Yet we know that it's best to forgive others, just as we, too, have been forgiven.

If there exists even one person—including yourself—against whom you still harbor bitter feelings, it's time to forgive and move on. Bitterness and regret are not part of God's plan for you, but God won't force you to forgive others. It's a job that only you can finish, and the sooner you finish it, the better.

If you are caught up in intense feelings of anger or resentment, you know all too well the destructive power of these emotions. How can you rid yourself of these feelings? First you must prayerfully ask God to cleanse your heart. Then you must learn to catch yourself whenever thoughts of bitterness or hatred begin to attack you. Your challenge is this: Learn to resist negative thoughts before they hijack your emotions. When you learn to direct your thoughts toward more positive topics, you'll be protected from the spiritual and emotional consequences of bitterness...and you'll be wiser, healthier, and happier too.

More from God's Word

*You have heard it said, "Love your neighbor
and hate your enemy." But I tell you, love your
enemies and pray for those who persecute you,
that you may be sons of your Father in heaven.*
MATTHEW 5:43–45 NIV

*My dear brothers and sisters, always be willing
to listen and slow to speak. Do not become angry
easily, because anger will not help you live
the right kind of life God wants.*
JAMES 1:19–20 NCV

*If anyone claims, "I am living in the light,"
but hates a fellow believer,
that person is still living in darkness.*
1 JOHN 2:9 NLT

*Everyone must be quick to hear, slow to speak,
and slow to anger, for man's anger does not
accomplish God's righteousness.*
JAMES 1:19–20 HCSB

*Do not be conquered by evil,
but conquer evil with good.*

ROMANS 12:21 HCSB

More Thoughts about Bitterness

He who cannot forgive others breaks the bridge over which he himself must pass.

CORRIE TEN BOOM

Bitterness is a spiritual cancer, a rapidly growing malignancy that can consume your life. Bitterness cannot be ignored but must be healed at the very core, and only Christ can heal bitterness.

BETH MOORE

Bitterness imprisons life; love releases it.

HARRY EMERSON FOSDICK

Bitterness is anger gone sour, an attitude of deep discontent that poisons our souls and destroys our peace.

BILLY GRAHAM

Revenge easily descends into an endless cycle of hate and violence. The Bible says never repay evil with evil.

BILLY GRAHAM

27

The Question

I can talk to God, but I have trouble waiting
for His answers. What does the Bible say
about listening to God?

The Answer

Whether you are communicating with God
or with other people, the Bible reminds us time
and again that it's always a good idea
to listen more than you talk.

*The purpose of all prayer is to find God's will
and to make that our prayer.*

CATHERINE MARSHALL

Be Still and Listen

Be still, and know that I am God.
PSALM 46:10 KJV

God speaks to us in different ways at different times. Sometimes He speaks loudly and clearly. But more often He speaks in a quiet voice—and if you are wise, you will be listening carefully when He does. To do so, you must carve out quiet moments each day to study His Word and to sense His direction.

Are you willing to pray sincerely and then to wait quietly for God's response? Can you quiet yourself long enough to listen to your conscience? Are you attuned to the subtle guidance of your intuition? Hopefully so. Usually God refrains from sending His messages on stone tablets or city billboards. More often He communicates in subtler ways. If you sincerely desire to hear His voice, you must listen carefully, and you must do so in the silent corners of your quiet, willing heart.

More from God's Word

Rest in the LORD, and wait patiently for Him.
PSALM 37:7 NKJV

Be silent before Me.
ISAIAH 41:1 HCSB

The one who is from God listens to God's words. This is why you don't listen, because you are not from God.
JOHN 8:47 HCSB

In quietness and in confidence shall be your strength.
ISAIAH 30:15 KJV

*Listen, listen to me, and eat what is good,
and you will delight in the richest of fare.
Give ear and come to me; listen that you may live.*
ISAIAH 55:2–3 NIV

More Thoughts
about Listening to God

When God speaks to us,
He should have our full attention.

BILLY GRAHAM

Prayer is not monologue, but dialogue.
God's voice in response to mine
is its most essential part.

ANDREW MURRAY

Deep within the center of the soul is a chamber
of peace where God lives and where,
if we will enter it and quiet all the other sounds,
we can hear His gentle whisper.

LETTIE COWMAN

If you, too, will learn to wait upon God, to get alone
with Him, and remain silent so that you can hear
His voice when He is ready to speak to you,
what a difference it will make in your life!

KAY ARTHUR

God's voice is still and quiet and easily buried
under an avalanche of clamor.

CHARLES STANLEY

28

The Question

I don't want to be spiritually stuck.
I want to keep growing and maturing
as a Christian. How can I do it?

The Answer

Spiritual maturity is a journey, not a destination.
You can, and should, continue to mature in your
faith through every stage of life. To do so, you
must ask for God's help and follow His instructions.
When you do your part, He'll certainly do His part.

*Although no single factor can guarantee
long-term recovery, spirituality has proven
to aid both adults and adolescents
in the process of overcoming addiction.*

DOUGLAS COOK, MD

Growing through and beyond Addiction

God blesses the people who patiently endure testing. Afterward they will receive the crown of life that God has promised to those who love him.

JAMES 1:12 NLT

Addiction, like other traumatic experiences, can ultimately lead to spiritual growth. When the addict turns to God for strength—and when healing takes place—growth inevitably occurs.

As a Christian, you should never stop growing. No matter your age, no matter your circumstances, you have opportunities to learn and opportunities to serve. Wherever you happen to be, God is there, too, and He wants to bless you with an expanding array of spiritual gifts. Your job is to let Him.

The path to spiritual maturity unfolds day by day. Through prayer, through Bible study, through silence, and through humble obedience to God's Word, we can strengthen our relationship with Him. The more we focus on the Father, the more He blesses our lives. The more carefully we listen for His voice, the more He teaches us.

In the quiet moments when we open our hearts to the Lord, the Creator who made us keeps remaking us. He gives us guidance, perspective, courage, and strength. And the appropriate moment to accept these spiritual gifts is always the present one.

More from God's Word

*Grow in the grace and knowledge of our
Lord and Savior Jesus Christ. To Him be the glory
both now and forever. Amen.*

2 PETER 3:18 NKJV

*Let us stop going over the basic teachings about
Christ again and again. Let us go on instead
and become mature in our understanding.*

HEBREWS 6:1 NLT

*Leave inexperience behind, and you will live;
pursue the way of understanding.*

PROVERBS 9:6 HCSB

*Endurance must do its complete work, so that you
may be mature and complete, lacking nothing.*

JAMES 1:4 HCSB

*I remind you to fan into flames
the spiritual gift God gave you.*

2 TIMOTHY 1:6 NLT

More Thoughts
about Spiritual Growth

*God's ultimate goal for your life on earth
is not comfort but character development.
He wants you to grow up spiritually
and become like Christ.*

RICK WARREN

*The vigor of our spiritual life will be
in exact proportion to the place
held by the Bible in our life and thoughts.*

GEORGE MUELLER

Mark it down. You will never go where God is not.

MAX LUCADO

*God will help us become
the people we are meant to be,
if only we will ask Him.*

HANNAH WHITALL SMITH

29

The Question

My addiction has caused me so many problems.
The pain I'm feeling seems like it will never end.
Where can I find hope?

The Answer

God can heal your pain, and He can heal your
addiction if you admit your helplessness and turn
everything over to Him. Be patient, be prayerful,
and be faithful.

Grace shines radiantly through addiction.
GERALD MAY, MD

Addiction and Grace

God, who is rich in mercy, because of His great love that He had for us, made us alive with the Messiah even though we were dead in trespasses. You are saved by grace!

EPHESIANS 2:4–5 HCSB

God's grace is sufficient to meet our every need. No matter our circumstances, no matter our personal histories, the Lord's precious gifts are always available. All we need to do is form a personal, life-altering relationship with His only begotten Son, and we're secure, now and forever.

Grace is unearned, undeserved favor from God. His grace is available to each of us. No sin is too horrendous, no behavior too outrageous, no addiction too destructive to separate us from God's love. We are saved by grace through faith. Jesus paid for our sins on the cross, and when we trust completely, God pronounces us "not guilty" of our transgressions.

Have you accepted Christ as your king, your shepherd, and your savior? If so, you are protected now and forever. If not, this moment is the appropriate time to trust God's Son and accept God's grace. It's never too soon, or too late, to welcome Jesus into your heart. And it's never too soon, or too late, to follow in His footsteps on the road to recovery.

More from God's Word

We have redemption in Him through His blood,
the forgiveness of our trespasses, according to the
riches of His grace that He lavished on us with all
wisdom and understanding.

Ephesians 1:7–8 HCSB

By grace you have been saved through faith,
and that not of yourselves; it is the gift of God,
not of works, lest anyone should boast.

Ephesians 2:8–9 NKJV

He gives us more grace. That is why Scripture says:
"God opposes the proud but gives grace
to the humble."

James 4:6 NIV

Grow in the grace and knowledge of our Lord
and Savior Jesus Christ. To Him be the glory,
both now and to the day of eternity.

2 Peter 3:18 NASB

My grace is sufficient for you,
for my power is made perfect in weakness.

2 Corinthians 12:9 NIV

More Thoughts
about God's Grace

*God's grace is just the right amount
of just the right quality arriving
as if from nowhere at just the right time.*

BILL BRIGHT

*Grace is the free, undeserved goodness
and favor of God to mankind.*

MATTHEW HENRY

*God's grace is His unmerited favor toward
the unworthy, by which He delivers them
from condemnation and death.*

JOHN MACARTHUR

Immerse yourself in the curriculum of grace.

MAX LUCADO

*The will of God will never take us where
the grace of God cannot sustain us.*

BILLY GRAHAM

30

The Question

Seems like everything is changing in my life and I'm searching for a renewed sense of purpose. How can I discover God's purpose for my life?

The Answer

God's plans for you are unfolding day by day. Keep your eyes and your heart open and let Him lead. Remaining addiction free is part of God's plan for you, so stay strong and walk with the Lord. He'll guide you along a path that's right for you.

You will show me the path of life;
in Your presence is fullness of joy;
at Your right hand are pleasures forevermore.
PSALM 16:11 NKJV

Rediscovering Your Purpose

*We have also received an inheritance in Him,
predestined according to the purpose of the One
who works out everything in agreement
with the decision of His will.*

EPHESIANS 1:11 HCSB

If you're recovering from addiction, you may be searching for a new direction, a renewed sense of purpose. If that's the case, you can take comfort in the fact that God doesn't do things by accident. He didn't put you here by chance or deliver you to your particular place, at this particular time, with your particular set of talents and opportunities on a whim. He has a plan, a one-of-a-kind mission designed especially for you. Discovering that plan may take time. But if you keep asking God for guidance, He'll lead you along a path of His choosing and give you every tool you need to fulfill His will.

Of course, you'll probably encounter a few impediments as you attempt to discover the exact nature of God's purpose for your life. And you may travel down a few dead ends along the way. But if you keep searching, and if you genuinely seek the Lord's guidance, He'll reveal His plans at a time and place of His own choosing.

Today and every day, God is beckoning you to hear His voice and follow His plan. When you listen—and when you answer His call—you'll be amazed at the wonderful things that an all-knowing, all-powerful God can do.

More from God's Word

*We must do the works of Him who sent Me while
it is day. Night is coming when no one can work.*
JOHN 9:4 HCSB

*Whatever you do, do it heartily,
as to the Lord and not to men.*
COLOSSIANS 3:23 NKJV

*We are His creation, created in Christ Jesus
for good works, which God prepared ahead
of time so that we should walk in them.*
EPHESIANS 2:10 HCSB

*We are God's coworkers.
You are God's field, God's building.*
1 CORINTHIANS 3:9 HCSB

*Whether you eat or drink,
or whatever you do,
do it all for the glory of God.*
1 CORINTHIANS 10:31 NLT